Praise for

TWELVE

How do we find something different within poetry today that isn't affected and trite? People are becoming more pretentious whilst proclaiming greater honesty; the more we share the less we are ourselves. Austin has her finger on the trigger when it comes to shaving the irrelevant and getting to the point. "You know what I think? I think forgiveness is infinitely intermittent, and real acceptance is bullshit." (Intermittent Bullshit).

If you're tired of reading Self-Help books that promote forgiveness and clean, easy recovery, then take a leaf from someone who has actually been there, and not with bleach and plastic gloves on. I'd quote nearly every poem in this book to illustrate reasons why it has to exist, but that would spoil so much, and I'd rather you discovered Kindra Austin's work for yourself.

—Candice Louisa Daquin, *Pinch the Lock*

Twelve is one of my favourite collections of the year, alongside Nicole Lyons' *Blossom and Bone*, and Austin's novel, *For You, Rowena*. It ranks up there among one of the most heartrending collections I've ever read. This is because *Twelve's* airtight narrative of bereavement gives you little breathing room against the barrage of Austin's grief over the death of her mother.

Overall, *Twelve* is a collection which reminds us death is not about the dead, but those who are left behind. In Austin's case, she has shaped it into a torch carried for hers, and wields it to light the dark ahead.

—Nicholas Gagnier, *Founding Fathers*

This book has overwhelmed me, it has slayed me with its truths. Those were the thoughts that came to mind after consuming her book. I don't use the word "consume" lightly: I ruminated as I read; her thoughts were nourishment for that part of me that ponders death. Yet I felt as if my heart had been splayed open: I didn't know if I should cry, or just bear witness. I admired and wondered yet again at Austin's willingness to reveal herself, her assuredness that her readers would catch those emotions and cradle them. That we could hold space for them, keep them safe, disperse them, or preserve them.

—Mariah Voutilainen, *Indie Blu(e)*

Praise for

Kindra M. Austin's debut book of poetry and prose,
Constant Muses

Upon opening Kindra M. Austin's *Constant Muses*, I was immediately taken with the noir-y feel of her poetry. As Austin's opening piece suggests, it is "eternally October" in the world that she paints with her rich verse. Skies are heavy with the weight of autumnal storms, the air thick with cigarettes, tongues dipped in bittersweet alcohol. Within this October specters lurk: female warriors, a mother with many faces, preserved memories. It is a séance in which the past is called up to hold hands with the present.

Austin's honest delivery and willingness to reveal her complex feelings, from distress and guilt to love and forgiveness, is generous and brave. It is this bravery and generosity that led me to re-read this book several times, peeling back layers to reveal the sources of such wonderfully emotional writing.

—Mariah Voutilainen, *Indie Blu(e)*

I have some of these poems memorized without trying—they stick under your skin and in your head that much. This book is amazing, and it's brilliantly split up with some extremely hard to stop reading prose. Kindra is special—she is not a cookie cutter poet. I don't think anyone could read her work without seeing her talent and falling in love straightaway.

—Georgia Park, *Quit Your Job and Become a Poet (Out of Spite!)*

Kindra's work isn't easy to pin down and explain. She's just got that SOMETHING that other writing usually doesn't have. That talent to write as if she's sitting right across from you, just talking, confessing, letting things out we all wish we could, or did when we had the chance. She's not like any other poet I've read. You'll see what I mean.

—Samantha Lucero, *Six Red Seeds*

ALSO BY KINDRA M. AUSTIN

POETRY

Constant Muses

FICTION

Magpie in August

For You, Rowena

TWELVE

Kindra M. Austin

© 2018 Kindra M. Austin
All rights reserved.
Cover design by Allane Sinclair

Printed in the United States of America.

No part of this book may be used, stored in a retrieval system, or transmitted in any form or in any means, or reproduced in any manner whatsoever without written permission from the author, except in the case of brief quotations used in reviews and critical articles.

Published by Blank Paper Press
Chesaning, MI

ISBN: 978-1-7328610-2-2

Library of Congress Control Number: 2018914003

In honor of my mother

"See ya later."

PROEM

She'd often made it difficult, but I did love my mom beyond measure. Before learning she had died, I don't believe I'd ever actually shrieked over any-fucking-thing in my life—that's saying a lot. On 8 November, 2017, at three-something in the afternoon, the sound that erupted from my lungs and out of my mouth was utterly empty, yet it carried a weight of pain that unequivocally transcends my comprehension to this day. The woman who gave birth to me—the woman I'd admired in the face of animosity, and who I'd always defended against abusers breathed no more.

I miss my mom's smile most of all. That genuine, life giving smile she had in spite of the shit she had to live with was...well, it was goddamned gorgeous. Her eyes, I swear, projected light when she was happy. My baby niece's eyes have that same magic—sweet babe born just six days before...

My mom was found in her apartment, a week dead. The police officer on the case had sternly suggested that my sister and I not go see her body. Although I had accepted straightaway that I wouldn't have to walk into a cold stainless steel room in the basement of a hospital to identify my mom's body, I felt the desire—no, the morbid need—to look upon her death.

In retrospect, I'm thankful for that officer's concern because I'd smelled the scent of my mom's decomposition lingering in her apartment, and I've recently read the autopsy report. Both were enough to remind me that sometimes, I'm still a smarty-pants little girl who believes she's entitled to know everything; and not everything is worth knowing.

TWELVE picks up where *Constant Muses* ends; this is the yearlong journey of my grief and healing expressed in poems and prose. While most pieces involve my mom directly, some are just byproducts of melancholy. But dark as my days have been, there is one who keeps me tethered to the light—you will know her influence in certain pieces; she reminds me to breathe on my worst days. And so I keep on digging into the pit of me—I know my truths deserve to be heard.

In *TWELVE*, you'll feel the mourning of a daughter, the love of a mother, and the highs, lows, and plateaus that make the healing process an intricate one. Above all, you'll feel the steel of a woman determined to hold on to life. To quote *The Crow*, one of my favorite films:

"It can't rain all the time."

Peace,

Kindra M. Austin, *TWELVE*

ACKNOWLEDGEMENTS

As always, I give thanks to:

Nicole, my darling daughter
Jim, my favorite husband
Tara, my devoted little sister
Andrea Walker, my bestie and favorite comedian.
Allane Sinclair, cover designer and my Kindred Spirit.

I owe immeasurable gratitude to my Sudden Denouement Literary Collective family. The writers at Sudden Denouement are indeed some of the best, most influential creators on the scene today. I'm truly blessed to know so many powerful, intimate writers who inspire me both creatively, and as a human being. To my brothers and sisters in writing:

Jimmi Campkin
Candice Louisa Daquin
Dennis Earley
Matthew D. Eayre
Rachel Finch
Nicholas Gagnier
Jasper Kerkau
Samantha Lucero
Nicole Lyons
Georgia Park
Marcia Weber
Christine E. Ray
Kristiana Reed
Mariah Voutilainen
Laurie Wise

Thank you, Mom.

CONTENTS

ix..........Dedication
xi..........Proem
xiii........Acknowledgments
3............Please Rewind
4............Until There's Nothing Left
5............Daisies: You Ain't Pushin 'Em
6............Blackness All Over the Bed
8............Sick
9............An Emotionless Affair
13.........Wake
14.........Thirty-Nine
15.........Supernova
16.........Center of Night
17.........Colossus
18.........Merry Christmas, Mother
19.........Intermittent Bullshit
20.........Rumination of a Eulogy
23.........Never Any Good at Math
24.........Rage with Me
25.........Blink
26.........Sorry I'm a Bitch
27.........Benders
28.........The Color of Beach Sand
31.........Recipient No Longer Exists
32.........A Peculiar Dream I Had
34.........Your Absence Is a Burglar
36.........You Said I was Happy

39..........My Love, I will Die for You
40..........In Waiting
41..........Chordae Tendineae
42..........Viscera in Danger (Revamp)
43..........Quest for Wellness
47..........Dead Mothers Don't Dine
49..........2 a.m.
50..........At the Dairy Case
51..........The Taste of My Grief
52..........Monochrome Lungs
55..........Happy Wives Bake Pies
56..........Slit Wrists and Hard Feelings
57..........Anyway, Always
59..........Mother Lioness
60..........For My Truest of Loves
61..........You Remind me
62..........Meditation
65..........Last Judgment
67..........Dreadful
68..........Marbles
69..........Head Over Heels
70..........Hellfire
71..........Numb
75..........I Knew My Worth
76..........Alcoholics Unanonymous
77..........Day Walkers and Night Terrors
78..........The Death of You
81..........Someone Told Me I Was Queen
82..........I Breathe, Still
83..........Wedding Poem
85..........The Air I Breathe
89..........I Can Love September
90..........Zero
91..........Eating Dirt

92..........What I Am
93..........Truth: The Liquid Kind
97..........I Don't Fear the Reaper
98..........Heart Misplaced
99..........For Magpie
100........Twelve
105........The Hated Eighth
106........A Scene I Desire
107........I Go On Because I Do

There will never be enough pages.

November

Why are you dead?

Please Rewind

Be kind, please rewind—
Mercy take me backward, back
to that night, damp black
when my heart did beat untouched
and the prospect of pain was
all I had.

Mercy take me back
to the night we met—
when your spectre not born yet
remained a prospect.

Be kind, please rewind—
Mercy take me backward, back…

I can only wander now
with poor pockets and
an empty rib cage.

Until There's Nothing Left

My heart itches in the dark, and I can hear a
scratching—
sounds like millions of insects marching
over a coffin.

I want to make my fingers into tiny shovels—
dig until there's nothing left.

Daisies: You Ain't Pushin 'Em

You've been condensed; 58
years reduced to granules and packed in plastic.
How badly I want to pick through the pieces and
find your teeth;
I wish to see your smile—not in a fucking
photograph, or mixed within
images
projected in my dreams.

Blackness All Over the Bed

It was easy to break her marinating heart on a Friday night when she was sat at the candle-lit kitchen table, chain-smoking and listening to Janis Joplin, or The Eagles, or Rod Stewart; sometimes I didn't, but most times I did because the tone of my voice, or the choice of my words, or the sound of my lungs breathing poisonous air reminded her of my dad. She'd always taught me to be honest, but never liked it when I was honest in the dim firelight encircled by her blackness. The blackness was viscous like the bile she'd vomit after everything else had come up at 3 a.m.

I found her once in the bathroom when I was fourteen years old, passed out in a pool of rejected alcohol, and I left her there, half-hoping she'd asphyxiate. I packed a duffel bag that late afternoon, and ran away with my best friend. We were only gone a few hours; I was relieved to come home and find my mother alive in her bed, heavily asleep.

I can't believe I'd left my sister. I don't recall the specifics of that day, but shit must have been head deep, because I cannot imagine abandoning Tara.

Tara. I've always looked after her, but now that our mother is gone, the responsibility I feel is heavier than ever. Taking care of my sister is something that's always been expected of me. I don't mean like, "hold her hand on your way to school." I mean legit parenting. But we're both adults, so that makes the weight all the more cumbersome. And Tara, she's a fierce woman. She doesn't need me to parent her, nor does she want me to. But habits are called habits for good reason. I don't think I'll ever be able to relinquish the charge of looking after my sister.

Even though I'm tired.

I'm so fucking tired.

My mother was tired when she died. However, I don't think she was so tired that she was ready to go away. She'd just welcomed a new granddaughter into the world. And her oldest granddaughter is getting married this summer. My mother was tired, but she was also looking forward to so much. I was looking forward to so much; over the past couple of years, she and I had made huge steps towards healing our relationship. She'd cut down significantly on her drinking, and I'd begun to see more of the mother I knew before alcoholism took hold of her. So now, I just feel fucking robbed.

Two nights ago, I was cooking dinner, and thinking of my mother. I had to stop what I was doing, I was so overcome. I went into my bedroom, and screamed until my throat went hoarse.

Then I threw up blackness all over the bed.

Sick

Most memories of you
taste like an utterance of vomit,
and I'm sick tonight
over you.
You'd raised an asshole, and
I'm furious I was
forced to be.

Now,
I can't miss you
without feeling like a goddamned phony—
without berating myself
for all the times I'd loved you
toughly.

I'm sick tonight
over the loss of you.

An Emotionless Affair

What you think you know of me, you've gleaned from pages of a yellow legal pad stained with sterile ink leaked from your doctor's pen; it's an emotionless affair, the goings-on between patient and psychiatrist. I'm a mistress in hysterics seeking validation from just another goddamned man. If this were the nineteenth century, you'd have long sent me to an asylum, and had my womb mutilated by staff surgeons.

When I speak, you scribble, and I imagine you're only illustrating me naked, sprawled upon the divan, jaundice skinned and lined with blue. Make me a whole person, you write (mocking me) inside a comic book word bubble inserted above my over-sized head. But I continue talking about how I feel since learning my mother had woken up dead, and the gut-raping grief inside of me, because I do want to be a whole person.

It's an emotionless affair, the goings-on between patient and psychiatrist.

And my imagination is a distrustful cunt.

December

Wake

You come to me often, and I can't take it—seeing your Cheshire smile, and glittering eyes. I'd thought dreams of you would bring me peace, but those visions of you animated, and the dulcet tones of your voice, well-remembered, bouncing against the walls of my skull only cause me agony.

I hold a wake with a devastated rib cage, fractured from the distension of a lamenting heart—my heart, it heaves, weeping tears of its own, crimson.

Thirty-Nine

I woke up stupid this morning, expecting a text.

What's the point of a birthday,
if you can't even fucking say thanks
to your mother?

I'll fall asleep tonight by the light of the lava lamp
you gave me last year.
When I was thirty-eight, and
you were alive.

Supernova

Pulverized, and expelled, am I
Intergalactic vomit, projectile—
Yes, I've achieved Supernova
Crimson crystalline bleeds sharp, and
Darts insurmountable space
I am particles one billion,
Undetected by naked
Eyes of infants, innocent

Center of Night

I remember everything, a curse in
center of night,
when cat stares through me, and
clock tick-tocks
witching hour is nigh
I wait cos I remember every scene
unseen with eyes mine, a curse in
center of night
I miss you most

Colossus

Night

I find solace in the frightening night, when the silence is amplified, and I am alone; I can hear my heart beating, and this war drum reminds me that I still breathe. My shadow is cast—hurled against dead buildings.

I smile, because for a moment, I am Colossus.

I make like a conqueror, and stomp my winter feet—the tantrum ricochets, scaring up phantoms that bellow in the moonlight.

I smile, because for a moment, I am Colossus, untouchable.

Merry Christmas, Mother

I scream Merry Christmas into blackness; and the blackness is Outer Space, where sounds are stillborn. I shudder under death lighted silver and blue.

I scream Merry Christmas.

Intermittent Bullshit

You were goddamned gorgeous, and a fucking conundrum, my mother. When I think of all the men in your life who'd tried to solve your riddles, I laugh. The relics of those men inhabit a corner in the catacombs of my heart. I don't want them, but each one retains a precious part of you, so there they shall remain. Yes, I'll keep those tokens to remind me that I never want to be like you—insecure.

You'd always believed you required a man's love in order to be completely happy. From the depths of my being, I am so sorry you'd lived your life on the cusp of a chasm so black. I wish you had known your true self through the eyes of your daughters; and I don't understand why Tara and I weren't reasons enough for you to be content.

I'm angry tonight—angry about your failures as a mother. And I'm pissed off at myself for even thinking about all of the men you'd put in front of me and my sister. You're fucking dead—anger is a waste of my energy. What kills me is that I'd believed this shit was behind me. I'd forgiven you a long time ago. So why am I reflecting on my adolescence all over again?

You know what I think? I think forgiveness is infinitely intermittent, and real acceptance is bullshit.

Rumination of a Eulogy

Yesterday marked one month since Tara and I held your memorial service; but as I was a captive, yet again clamped between the jaws of a Fibromyalgia flare-up, I was unable to give 26 November the thoughtfulness that day does deserve. Today, I'm well enough to consider all of the words I'd spoken when I eulogized you.

Admittedly, I hadn't prepared an oration. Was it because I would avoid the task at every opportunity, or that I'd actually believed I could do you truer justice with improvising?

Both. But I suppose it doesn't matter, because I'm glad I didn't write up something (pretentious). Had I written a eulogy, it would have undoubtedly come out affected.

Everything I said about you is the bare truth—in life, you never decked your head in laurels. You always worked hard, and all you'd ever wanted out of the goddamned deal was to raise two happy daughters, and keep them out of poverty. Your heart never did need dressing up, Mom.

I'm at peace with the words I'd chosen; though there's no real repose for my fragmented soul.

I fucking miss you.

And I love you, endlessly.

January

Never Any Good at Math

Something happens, and I am reminded that
all of the good words have been taken by the 80s.

I can't write you a heavy synth song, penned in black kohl;
can't dip my heart into inderivative hair dye—
there's no such thing, really.

Something happens, and I am reminded that
I can't call you.

Something happens, and I am reminded that
I can't hug you.

Something happens, and I remember that
I'd forgotten to miss you for 5 whole fucking minutes.

There are 300 seconds in 5
fucking minutes, and
3,600 seconds in 1 hour,
which means there are 86,400 seconds in 24 hours,
or 1,440 minutes in a goddamned day.
All of that translates to a lot of fucking time spent
forgetting to remember you're dead.

And I can't write you a love song.

Rage with Me

I'm just a mad girl,
Looking for some hips to bump
Hips against.
Rage with me, will you?
I've gotta mama complex—
Keeps me outta shape, and
I could use the exorcise.

Blink

Who do I speak to
in the dark,
when my moon is
encumbered
by intransient clouds?
Selene,
can you hear me?

Blink twice for
yes.

Sorry I'm a Bitch

I'm cruel—
too cool for school.
I don't even want your lunch money—
happy to beat you up for free.
Besides, your heart has always been
nourishment enough for me.
Slice through the muscle like
you're carving rare beef, and
serve it on the bone china
I'd fashioned from your rib cage.

I'm sorry I think
when I drink
too much.

Benders

Don't have benders;
Gotta mutha-fuckin
NASCAR track.
Drive that oval at
two-twenty for days.
Look, Mom—
I made the Hall of Fame,

Just below your name.

The Color of Beach Sand

We had you pushed into the furnace;
spoiling organs and
leaking skin were
burned away.
Your pulverized bones
resemble beach sand in
Tawas,
fittingly.

Abandoned the wagon
again,
Cos I'm a goddamned tyrant,
missing you, Mother—
been consuming for two
twelve hours, and I
will continue to imbibe until my barbican
heart has been razed.
This early morning,
trust,
I'll make it to market by noon—
I learned how to function from you.

Mother,
are you proud of me,
still?
I ask your ashes kept in
keepsake urns. Ashes—
granules, the color of
beach sand.

February

Recipient No Longer Exists

Your invitation has been rescinded—
no justice
inside a.m.
Name stricken from the guest list just this
mourning,
cos you don't have a thing to wear.

Today, Nicole asked me to email her the wedding guest list so she and her fiancé can work on finalizing the count, and begin mailing invitations. I looked it over to make sure I wasn't missing anyone before hitting send.

I was missing someone. I was missing you, Mom.

I highlighted your name and address. And I cried. I hit delete. And I cried.

I cried yesterday, too. Nicole had selected the most beautiful wedding dress—she looks like an absolute doll in it. I took loads of photos of her standing on the pedestal before a three-way mirror. I was so excited, I attached the images to a string of text messages. Then I remembered you wouldn't receive them.

You no longer exist.

A Peculiar Dream I Had

I dreamt you were a naked doll, sized true-to-life. You were assembled like the art manikin I use for sketching, only your head was your actual head—your face was arranged in a placid expression. A random little girl had fished you out of a cold river, and I snatched you from her greedy arms as she was celebrating her catch.

"She's too big for you," I cried. Cradling you, I carried you away from the shore lowly lit by a dull sun, and into the damp grey woods. I was chased by faceless men who wanted you, and I heard the little girl lamenting. "Fuck you! She's mine," I kept yelling. "You can't have my mother!"

And in a blink, you were alive, penned in a clearing by a circle of strangers. You were dressed in a red shirt, and faded blue jeans. I couldn't make out the silent words rushing from your mouth. I could only pay attention to the man with a sword. You were murdered in front of me. I saw the long blade enter you through your back— through your thoracic spine.

The death scene repeated like cruelly spliced film. I watched your face fade away and reappear again and again, for an immeasurable space of time, until the phone began to ring.

Stood in the driveway of our house in Lapeer, I kicked at the loose stones, waiting for the ringing to stop.

TWELVE/Kindra M. Austin

"It's for you," said someone lounging in the bed of a pickup truck. An unrecognizable guy with long, dirty blond hair. I took the tan receiver, and pressed it against my aching head.

"I love you. I miss you so much, Mom." I knew it was you. And I knew you were dead.

I know you are dead.

There was a long, crackling silence that made my brain itch.

Then you said, "I think of you all the time."

Your Absence Is a Burglar

I'm running out of poetry; your Absence is a burglar of words and rhythm. You're the one who'd always told me to write my heart out. Just write, baby girl. Tell me, how am I supposed to cope with the loss of my goddamned verses? Who am I, if not a writer?

***

I wandered way down cobblestone,
deep in fog exhaled from lungs.
Mourning mind preoccupied,
my flitting feet followed instinct—
landed me at Dimwit dive-bar,
Old Town.
Somehow,
I ended up supping a ginny Gin Rickey.

Stood
in the nook at the
billiards table, a beatnik boy-toy of
Nimoy stature floated me a
hawk-eye look; affixed a fag to
his bottom lip, and
I just knew he was the type who
liked
Wuthering fucking Heights.

***

What comes next? I have an idea, but can't seem to execute it. I've been staring at this piece of shit for five wasted days. I'm too consumed with thoughts of you. And damn it, I'd like to be able to write about some other things now and again—in between fits of losing my mind over visions of you alone on the kitchen floor, and your blank eyes staring into nothingness. Shit, I'd like to put head to pillow at night without having to recall the scent of death that cleaved to your apartment despite the bottles of bleach that were used to clean up your leaked fluids.

Mother, what am I supposed to do? I'm so fucking tired of writing about you.

But who am I, if not a writer?

TWELVE/Kindra M. Austin

<u>You Said I Was Happy</u>

And I was when
I was not.
I was not...

You thought you spoke magic;
I believed, too.

Then I woke up a woman who knew.

March

My Love, I Will Die for You

mon amour, je vais mourir pour toi

Hand me the scalpel;
I will
excise my own love
muscle,
98.6° and sputtering crimson
motor oil.

I want to see my cooling lifeblood
soak into the pores of your gluttonous hands; and
when you comb those sticky fingers through your dark
curled hair, I
want you to remember my kohl edged eyes staring down
at you in the
darkness of our vulgar fornication.
Bite into the piece of me you cradle in red slickened
palms, and
sup what's left of my liquid soul.

In Waiting

I waited at the back of his throat—
waited to hear him confess my name so I could come out
from behind his teeth, and defend my claim
over him. Illusory love o' mine
kept me cleaving to the bitter of his tongue; for all of her
disdain he swallowed, I did
wash in, waiting.

We used to get shit-faced, and fuck each other mad,
down by the river in
dew slick grass,
monstrous 'neath the white-gold moon.

He'd give it to me good 'til I was
howling, and scratching
bloodstained nails at that discerning watch
slung up high in sleeping cerulean.

I waited at the back of his throat—
waited for him to confess my name.
He didn't.

Every time he chokes, he's reminded of me.

Chordae Tendineae

Pluck me a melody from the sinews of your heart—
be mine
own Orpheus; private poet,
sing me your soul.
Tell me you'll give me adoration, heavy—
more than mine arms can carry,
plus.

I promise I will dance for you like
Eurydice,
cherished wife.

I promise I will strip for you like
prostitutes do,
but for the low, low price of
one true sweetheart.

Pluck me a melody from the sinews of your heart
when I wake up bathing
in mine
own vomit, cos I gone and done it
again—
got stupid
over the love of a lyre.

My mother,
a perpetual Eurydice

Viscera in Danger (revamp)

Their need is visceral. Oh!
Pretty blonde girl,
fresh trailer park trash,
junkyard dogs snarl and quarrel over your flesh—
tongues wag to get at your bones.
Twelve years old, and
your marrow is aromatic.

Mother's a full-time drunk, and you
only got a part-time daddy.

Good luck, baby;

Welcome to Contaminated Manor.
Find your place in the Court somehow
without
letting them taste you.

Quest for Wellness

Obsessive Compulsive Disorder

Intrusive

Thoughts take hold of my hand, and
lead me across the street where
shades who are, and have yet to be
sing
ring-around-the-rosie whilst
dancing in the daylight—
so bold have they grown to
stray away from night.

What medicine exists
this
side of death that can save me?

Every day I armor myself in
quest for wellness.

See the fire in my footprints.

April

Dead Mothers Don't Dine

I dreamt I was miniature, traveling through a labyrinthine trailer park diseased with taupe colored muck, and flip-flopping mudskippers; pectoral fins glimmered in waves, despite the sunless, flat grey ceiling of a sky. My skin screamed at the loathsome goby touch, and my mouse heart beat savagely against its cage.

Panic drove my legs, and then I was airborne, peddling.

I just knew I'd make it home.

Touching down in a blue sky town dressed in purple hued Victorian architecture, my height increased with every footstep; I kept growing until I reached 5 feet, 6 ¾ inches. I walked past a liquor store that also sold Native American folk art, and was reminded of you. The booze bottles displayed in the front window sparkled in the sunlight like your eyes did, once upon a time in another plane of reality.

Fade out...

Fade in...

I attend an outdoor Thanksgiving dinner.

The grass is long, soft, and deep green—so lovely beneath my bare feet. A long table is sat atop a small hill; a plump, silver haired woman wearing a powder blue house dress is arranging place settings. I see your name card. Your plate has been placed upside down, and your napkin,

folded, at the left. There are no utensils, or a chalice set for you.

Dead mothers don't dine.

2 a.m.

You worked third shift when I was in high school, and sometimes you'd stay out of the bar after work on a Friday. You'd come home to pick up Tara and me, and we'd all go grocery shopping at Farmer Jack. I wish I could remember exactly why you and I always ended up laughing so hard that other customers would give us dirty looks. The dirty looks only made us laugh louder.

What I do know for certain is that you were good for encouraging my outrageous jokes and awful clown behavior. The harder you laughed, the harder I'd press, and that's how it had always been with you and me. The sound of your laughter was my drug, and that's one reason why we needed each other so much.

After shopping, we'd go to the diner. You'd usually order fish and chips, but on occasion chose the hot beef sandwich; Tara and I would regularly get hot turkey sandwiches with mashed potatoes and gravy. I'd eat all of mine, Tara would mutilate her plate into an ugly mess not worth keeping, and you'd take half of yours home in a box.

At the Dairy Case

Fuck grocery store etiquette.
Tears for Fears tells me to shout, so I let it all out
in front of the dairy case while inspecting my
perfection—
mourning after reflection—in the fingerprinted glass.
My cheeks are hollow
but my gut is bloated
from too much diet soda (I'm watching my figure) and
vodka.

In front of the dairy case, blocking access to the skim
milk,
I let it all out,
and I like the way
my pretty mouth contorts
into a beastly maw
when I cry.

The Taste of My Grief

Today my tongue tastes yellow, not like lemons, but like nicotine stained fingertips, or young pus on the cusp of turning pea green. That's what it is—my tongue tastes like infection. Tastes like your moldering death and sticky linoleum. Tastes like November 8th, the day I learned you'd died in that goddamned apartment with no one to mourn you but your fucking cat. It comes out of nowhere and somewhere both at once, this yellow sick. It begins in my belly, and travels upward through my esophagus, coating my mouth. Bile, oil viscous. Yes, this is the taste of my grief.

Monochrome Lungs

Today my eyes are monochrome lenses through which I deride;
derailed by your present absence, I do despise
this goddamned neighborhood.
The people all breathe too loudly,
showing off their functioning lungs.

May

Happy Wives Bake Pies

The
sun
came begging again
at my doorstep; I turned him
away. Got no use for gods at play.
Too much decease has grown me up.
I am weeds, immune to
disease, and I only live
in order to survive.
But to what end?
So questions
Depression,
mine. Depression
is the paparazzi—
always trying to catch
me crazy, display me
for eyes, judgmental.
Mental Health Care
is a one line joke.
I am weeds, and I
fucking choke
behind lips
upturned,
lovely.

Slit Wrists and Hard Feelings

I'm sorry for my reply way back when
you were downing, and
drowning in sick—
the stigma your upbringing had
convinced you was actual.
You'd phoned your mother that night,
only to be answered with phony Christian
scripture.
But what I'd said was worse;

You could have had the decency to do it where my little
sister wouldn't find you.

We'd almost lost you
twenty-one years ago;
you knew
what you were doing with that knife.
And you knew
what you could do
the second time you'd turned to the kitchen drawer
for relief.

Anyway, Always

Thinking about it now, I'm not the least bit
sorry for the hateful shit I'd said to you
eleventy years ago, when I was a kid
and you fucking knew better.
I rescind my apologies.
Not that my sorries ever meant a good
goddamn to you, anyway—
they were ever only as true as your own,
anyway.

Insincerity: a common factor.

No, that's not true…the truth is complex.

I wish I hadn't apologized so much for defending myself
against you.

And I wish you hadn't rolled over so easily whenever
I called you out. I wish you'd properly raged against
the reasons you were the way you were. Sure,
you'd spoken of the ghosts that breathed inside of you—
warned me of them—but never did you
exorcise them. Never did you make them scream in
terror.

Not that your armor went unused.
You'd fought your best all your life…

I am greater than you had ever hoped to be.
I've welded your chainmail to my own,

and I am running into battle
with your heart sewn into my banner.

Mother mine, I know your truths; yours are mine,
and I will defend them,
always.

I will make your ghosts and mine scream in terror.

Mother Lioness

I wonder, Mother,
had you ever
felt
just one hot moment
when you knew for a fact that
you were fierce as
fuck?

Mother Lioness, I miss you

For My Truest of Loves

The day was grey-blue, echo of your eyes;
sky filled up with promise of rain,
and we waited for beloved petrichor.
Lemon yellow and speckled black,
a noble friend
clasped
your flaxen strands and flexed its wings.
What dreams did she bring, my darling?
Do you know how often
I dream of the daylight that dances
upon your face?
Formed inside my body, you are
living art,
gusting love from
honest lungs—
you speak your truths.
Honor your heart always, baby girl,
and you'll always be rewarded with
self-respect.
Live kindly, and the butterflies will flock to you,
forever.

You Remind Me

You are droplets of sunlight in the midst of a rainstorm,
reminding me
the Constant breathes for me
when I am drowning.

You are the Roar when my words won't come—
speaking for me,
reminding me
I am never voiceless.

In this world disparaged by the Blight of divisiveness,
you are true Eden,
reverberating the vibrancy of the Righteous.
You remind me to love.

For you, I too, will be
Bender of Light,
Queen of this Jungle,
Garden of Peace.
I will remind you to love.

Meditation

Shall I ascend to solitude,
eagle high
enough to spy
myself?
Put my metal parts to practice, and
train my reason to speak in
comprehensive sentences?

I presently think in blinks of
tainted photographs
flicking—
our lives a fucking flip-book filled with phony
animation, as
though we've never been anything more than a
pair of paper dolls pretending to breathe.

The surgeon lied. I am not bionic;
should've demanded a synthetic heart
instead.
Mine is afflicted with fissures, and
I feel the blood leaching like so many earthworms
smothering my organs.

My body is not a temple, but a churchyard—
your burial ground, and there's no space reserved for
me. So ascend I shall,
eagle high
enough...

June

Last Judgement

Come on down from there,
if only for a quick minute.
The last time I saw you is
unsatisfactory in hindsight.
Retrospection is a bitch dressed in my skin—
I've become leprous.
I may not pray to God, but I do
talk to Jesus. My words
fall on dead ears.
Christ will not come to me.
And if only for a quick minute, you will not
come down from there.

***

Your mother keeps on ringing me.
I don't answer.
Does my cruelty hurt you terribly?
Some things I just can't do to honor you.
To answer is to satisfy Jehovah, and I do not
wish to please Him. He'd used her willing hands to
ruin you. I've decided that
forgiving trespasses does not heal me.
Leave the forgiving to God.
Some things are simply
unforgivable
by the human heart.

***

You were both meaner and kinder than me.

TWELVE/Kindra M. Austin

I float about the in-between,
neither better nor worser.
Mother, how could you have
ever thought yourself
lesser than me?
You were my teacher—
the one who'd showed up
drunk every day,
but a teacher nonetheless.
And I wish you'd come down from there,
if only for a quick minute.

***

Come on down from there,
if only for a quick minute.
The last time I saw you is
unsatisfactory in hindsight.

Dreadful

I can't drive past a dead animal splayed and stinking on the side of the road in the summer heat without thinking of you. The tang you'd left behind inside your apartment is no different than a fucking stupid deer, rotting; we're all animals, after all. The similarity is incredibly depressing. Makes my mind wander into the macabre. I can't help but envision you hanged upside down and sliced open in some hillbilly pole barn with your entrails falling from your middle, and plunking into an orange Home Depot bucket.

I scold myself aloud: Don't think about that!

I can't help it. Intrusive Thoughts are a part of O.C.D.

You never knew that I live with this condition, and I'm glad I never told you. You had enough to worry about; you weren't mentally equipped to handle this sickness that colors me dreadful.

Marbles

Memories are marbles
banging against one another,
and bouncing off the walls of my skull.
I'm scrambled brains with a side of ketchup.

You were the same as I am.
Or I am the same as you were—
you're dead.

Dead. What an ugly word.
Dead. Dead.
DEAD.

My mother is dead.

Head Over Heels

I'm head over heels,
tied up and strangled
by my entrails—
my insides
excised—
you keep a terrific tongue
unleashed between liar's teeth
stained with victory and breast milk.
Man-child, I've never known a coward
quite like you. Your truth is treachery;
and it fucking guts me.
I'm head over heels
in disgust with you.

You've disrespected her memory.

Hellfire

You threaten me with fire—say you know
where I am going. The joke is on you,
cos I'm already burning
in my shoes,
cracking concrete
wide
fuckin-open.

<u>Numb</u>

I buried myself by the seaside 'neath a sky
patchwork grey and sobbing. Never in life had
I been so severely revered for my truths.
Posthumous respect is a backhanded compliment that
bleeds into my grave, cold and unimportant.
Ain't nothing much that matters to a corpse.

July

I Knew My Worth

I knew my worth when I was hot as fuck and
boys all lined up to
pet my cleft at the blind side of the playground—
dirty fingers
mercifully uneducated in the intricacies of
female anatomy

I knew my worth when I was hot as fuck in
middle school, despite my flat chest and
highly guarded cleft—
face of Helen and an ass that wouldn't quit,
by the gods, I knew my worth

I knew my worth when I was hot as fuck and
high school boys poorly educated in the delicacies of
female anatomy
petted my cleft with excavating fingers—
I sang hymns for my molested hymen

I knew my worth when I gave birth
two weeks before graduation, and I was in love;
my sweet babe, my savior—
she taught me the truth of my worth

<u>Alcoholics Unanonymous</u>

Hi.
I'm Kindra—alcoholic.
It's been thirsty seconds since my last drink, and
thirty nine years since my last confession.
I turn forty in December.
I've kissed a few girls,
dropped acid
once,
finger fucked myself eleventy hundred times, and
committed adultery with an Englishman
who won't leave me alone—
my pussy is lined with gold.
I smoke pot with my dad,
who abhors alcohol.

Hi.
I'm Kindra.
My mother was an alcoholic.
I don't know how many times she'd
finger fucked herself, or how many joints
she'd smoked while riding shot-gun with my dad.
I don't know if she'd ever dropped acid, or how many times
she might've wished she could confess to a god who'd forsaken her.
All I know is that her life isn't my problem—
I don't have to make amends on her behalf.
My name is Kindra, and I battle against alcoholism.

Day Walkers and Night Terrors

You won't appreciate the night until it rips you awake late in the afternoon; until it forces you to stare down the cold yellow sun. Then you'll know the day-walking ghosts—the ones who fraternize amongst parkland rose beds, unaware that their garden tea has aged one hundred plus years. These specters who sport ring-around-the-collar or cut-outs in their chests smile stupid at one another while the drink they swallow whizzes down between their legs like healthy streams of urine. At first you might think that ignorance isn't so bad; but as the sun begins to descend, necks will bow and chests will weep anew in recognition of reality. Lamenting will stir the twilight, and whisk the sky into black—you'll recognize the increasing heavy, and at the height of the Witching Hour, you will fathom the pain of a ghoul.

You will finally understand your own kind.

The Death of You

Tramadol Toxicity—
that's a real bitch-ity.
Surely
Narcotics
are dirty
Sarcastics?

High risk
for addiction
and dependence.
Can cause
respiratory
distress and
death   h
when   g
taken in   i
      h
         doses
or combined
with other
substances,
especially
alcohol.

You didn't mean to,
did you,
Mama?

August

TWELVE/Kindra M. Austin

<u>Someone Told Me I Was Queen</u>

Someone told me I was Queen of _____
So I hit the pavement with
nothing but the
shoes on my feet and
two middle fingers.

I followed black wings and
learned how to prey.
I communed with rivers and
willows and
winds of change.
I defied a mountain and
slept at its summit.
I made the day blush and
trained the night to genuflect.

Someone told me I was Queen of _____
So I hit the pavement with
nothing but the
shoes on my feet and
two middle fingers.

I returned home,
not Queen of fucking Nothing;
I returned
Commander of My Heart.

I Breathe, Still

For a minute or more, I was dead as you,
as you were technically dead
before the end was absolute—
before your brain conceded.
For a minute or more, my world was edged in
blossoming dark,
engrossing, on the cusp of consent.
Blackbirds congregated, chattered 'round my head, and
they called dibs on my vital organs—
heart, liver, kidneys, and lungs.
One expressed explicit interest in
my spleen—
keen student of human anatomy,
morbid corvid.
Then a cardinal came with your breath on its wings,
and I breathed.
I just breathed.
I breathe, still…

TWELVE/Kindra M. Austin

<u>Wedding Poem</u> *

Our loved ones who've risen
and live now in the bless-ed skies of rose gold—
they beam down upon you two,
as we all who breathe are
smiling upon your grand
unification.

This day, you've both chosen to
tie your souls together before devoted eyes.
We are all bless-ed
witnesses
to these oaths.
We are all bless-ed
to be in the presence of genuine love.

Nicole—
my sweetest girl,
I know you
as surely as I know the cadence of my heartbeat.
The first time I held you,
I knew
you were meant for me.

Now you're meant for him, too.

Isaiah—
young man of conviction,
I trust you
as surely as I trust the rhythm of my lungs.   ,
I know

your hands were meant for hers.
The journey has begun;

Go forth with Virtue of Truth in
mind,
mouth,
and deed.
Honor one another with Respect;
for weaved within its fabric are the
sinews of great character.

The journey has begun;

Go forth with all of our love and blessings.

Nicole and Isaiah Rodriguez—25 August, 2018

✱ I wrote this poem in tribute to my daughter and son-in-law, and also to honor those who attended the ceremony in spirit alone. My mother had been looking forward to seeing her first grandchild pledge her vows to the man she loves. Sadly, Isaiah had also lost his grandmother before the wedding.

The Air I Breathe

Tears go by as years expand from Heaven to horizon;
and I scale the mountain ranges risen in
consequence of your death.
Jesus, or some other guardian breathes for me
whilst my lungs delight in respite from high altitudes.

***

In this,
the winter of my youth,
stillness
settles deep into bone,
and I am reconciled.

As I prepare for sleep 'neath a blanket of white,
you visit upon me memories,
and I am happy here
at the summit of my youth;
for I will awaken in the dawn of golden age.

***

Tears go by as years expand from Heaven to horizon;
and I've dominated mountain ranges
risen in the pit of me—
all of them consequences of your death.
It was you who lent me breath.

September

I Can Love September

Summer is falling;
soon
clusters of jaundice,
rotten red apple, and gold-
fired colored leaves
will assemble at
my feet.

I remember
how pretty you looked when
clothed in
autumnal shades—
how the hues did praise
enchanted
eyes,
ever
changing.

Summer is falling;
you've no more birthdays—
no more suffering.

I can love September,
still.

Zero

I was fine yesterday,
but today is September 15—
another date to uncelebrate.
Your birthday doesn't total
no more.

Old age is a fable;
I was forced to stop counting at 58.
Today, you're supposed to be 59,
but instead you're fucking zero.

Zero.

Eating Dirt

Dirt in my mouth—
I'm still spitting grit.
I used to play in the driveway with my Big Foot
monster truck
while Mom and Dad argued in the kitchen;
their voices obliterated the window screen and
shattered my veins.
My bottom lip was always bleeding from
punctures pressed by top teeth, bunny sharp.
My skin was always sweating because my heart was
always howling.
I talked to people no one could see but me, and I was
frightened because they were real to no one else.
Sometimes they visit when I'm half-awake, ageless
faces reminding me that I'll never be
anything but small for as long as I breathe.
Sometimes they visit when I'm half-asleep, and
I wonder what my mother's ashes taste like.

What I Am

I am but paper,
gatherer of verses—
rip me
rip me
when I die.

Tear me
tear me into mouth sized
morsels.
Consume me
when I die;
Let me exist though I may not live.

Truth: The Liquid Kind

I listen to Radiohead
when I contemplate killing you—
I want to smash your glass and
get at the inside of your meaning.

Shells tell different truths—
look at me.
See,
I'm right and tight
with my plastic teeth,
and painted eyes that never blink.

We mislead, you and me.

October

I Don't Fear the Reaper

I fear being found.

Bloated,
Diffused Green, and
Rigor Mortis—

I fear screams I will not hear.

Let me be like cat or dog;
I'll run away from home to
land at
Death's doorstep.
Let me breakdown
unknown
and nurture the earth with quiet dignity.

I fear a face I will not see.

Bloated,
Diffused Green, and
Rigor Mortis—

I fear her grief.

Heart Misplaced

Thought I'd felt my heart stir.
Make my hands into shovels
and dig up the garden,
    again.

    Goddamned,
    I am.

There it is,
feeding the weeds.

TWELVE/Kindra M. Austin

<u>For Magpie</u>

August has come and gone again.

Summer leaves are falling down
drowsy in October;
still, and often harder now,

I remember true.

For you are she, and she is you.

Your legend lives in ciggie scented papers—
pages found all nearly read beside my mother's
vacant bed,
never to be finished.

I wait to see.

For I am Magpie, and she is me.

Twelve

Happy Halloween—
you've been dead
twelve months
            today.

                    ***

I'd been anticipating the second-coming of a mental breakdown. So far, I've only cried over your plants. Melvin chewed up some the leaves, and dug up the dirt. It's my fault because I'd forgotten to remove the pots from the windowsill before I went to bed last night. You know how naughty my guy can be when I'm asleep. I have no idea how you kept Jinx out of your plants for all those years.

So, there I was in the kitchen earlier this evening, frantically transplanting sections of your Heartleaf Philodendron, while trying to keep an eye on the dinner cooking on the stovetop. Potting soil littered the table, and as I was cleaning up, Jim came in, and hugged me.

"What are you doing?" he asked.

"Oh, just trying to save my mom. I had to move some of her to another pot."

"You know that's not your mom, right?"

I gasped, and I cried. I shook. Then I conceded, "I know!"

Jim held me tighter, and said, "I miss her, too. And she's not a plant. No matter what, we have her. We have her here with us."

I clutched his shoulders and he absorbed me.

***

Happy Halloween—
you've been dead
twelve months
         today.

Your presence is
alive and well;
no matter what,
we have you
here.

No Heartleaf
Philodendron could
contain you,
anyway.

November

You're not all gone.

The Hated Eighth

Linger;
Delores sings in a loop,
even though
she's dead now, too.

But,

I will keep my shit together
for my precious little sister,
on this day,
the hated eighth
              of November.

A Scene I Desire

The incandescent radiance
of a midnight living room
breathing heavily scented smoke...
sandalwood and roses with tobacco undertones,
menthol.

She's been thrown against the wall; I watch her shadow
bend 'round corners, taking the form of a cave dwelling
spider.

Elvis sings Suspicious Minds; and my mama
subscribes—
they can't go on together,
so she rearranges furniture,
as is her wont to rid his image.

I'm caught lurking in the hallway,
and she smiles.

She smiles.

A scene I desire to find again.

I Go On Because I Do

I go on because I do

like you
did
dare
the wind, with unfurled wings;
wield fire and raze lies

like you
did
dare
the resolve of demons;
spit spite then flash a wink

like you
did
dare
the makers of brick walls;
detonate dynamite

I go on because I do

like you
did
love
unquestionably;
there is solace to be found
within
the pages of your life
Though I'll never finish grieving,

TWELVE/Kindra M. Austin

your death will not define me;
and you
wouldn't have wished it so

I go on because I do

like you
did
love
unquestionably

About the Author

Kindra M. Austin is an indie author and editor from Chesaning, Michigan. She is the founder of Poems and Paragraphs, and co-founder of Blank Paper Press, and Indie Blu(e) Publishing. Her debut novel, *Magpie in August* was published in April, 2017, and her book of poems and prose titled *Constant Muses* followed in December. Her latest novel, *For You, Rowena* was released in August, 2018.

Other publications include several poems featured in *Anthology Volume I* (Writings from the Sudden Denouement Literary Collective), *Swear to Me*, and *All the Lonely People* (Free Verse Revolution), as well as two essays advocating for LGBTQ rights, printed in the Ohio Mansfield Pride magazine.

In November, 2018, Austin and Christine E. Ray, her publishing partner at Indie Blu(e), combined their talents with indie authors Candice Louisa Daquin (*Pinch the Lock*) and Rachel Finch (*A Sparrow Stirs Its Wings*) to produce *We Will Not Be Silenced: The Lived Experience of Sexual Harassment and Sexual Assault Told Powerfully through Poetry, Prose, Essay, and Art*.

Austin is presently working on her third novel, *Royce, with the Rose Gold Hair*, to be published by Blank Paper Press in summer of 2019.

www.ingramcontent.com/pod-product-compliance
Lightning Source LLC
Chambersburg PA
CBHW031449040426
42444CB00007B/1032